ROBERT HELPMANN

1. Helpmann as Hamlet

ROBERT HELPMANN

CHOREOGRAPHER

By
CARYL BRAHMS

Photographs by
RUSSELL SEDGWICK
(*of* TUNBRIDGE-SEDGWICK)

LONDON
B. T. BATSFORD, LTD.
15 North Audley Street, W.1

First Published Summer, 1943
Second Impression January, 1945

THE SADLER'S WELLS BALLET, drained by the war and working away from its own milieu and under unaccustomed conditions, has found a new choreographer of the first importance in its leading male dancer, Robert Helpmann.

Helpmann has been trained and developed solely in the Wells Company, save only for a little "fancy dancing" of a Saturday afternoon in his early Australian youth, and, later, foundation lessons with Novikov, at that time touring Australia with Anna Pavlova.

Helpmann has done a certain amount of work outside the company. He has danced in revue. He has appeared, and notably, in Shakespeare at the Old Vic. He has done an occasional film or a broadcast. He has made dance arrangements for West End shows. But these interludes have served only to send him back to the Ballet more eagerly.

Robert Helpmann was born in Australia on April 9th, 1909. His father is one of the leading judges of wool—no small distinction in that vast knowledgeable territory. His mother, the daughter of a pioneer, her days bounded by the polite Edwardian social round, longed always to go on the stage. How well she understood that same longing when she met it in her two children. Now her daughter is one of Australia's leading actresses and her son is a fine dancer and a virtuoso mime. He is also the most interesting choreographer we have had since Balanchine. Not through any vast mastery of the *pas*, as is to be found in the ballets of Fokine, Massine and Nijinska. How could this be with only three ballets in which to find it? Though in his third, least considerable, and, at the time of writing, latest ballet, *The Birds*, he shows an increasing command of the technique for extending the ballerina. Helpmann's interest lies rather in the dramatic content of the story that he has to tell. He brings drama to the ballet with a strong sure touch such as we find only in the work of Fokine. And because the influences that surround Helpmann are English influences his ballets have as national a flavour as Shakespeare's Falstaff—a subject that he must some day tackle.

Armed with his Fancy Dancing, Robert Helpmann made his first professional appearance in a musical comedy—*Frasquita* in which Marie Burke was playing the lead—in a Spanish dance "madly passionate and very energetic".

It was while he was appearing in the Christmas pantomime *Sinbad the Sailor*, in what must have been a very fascinating spectacle entitled "The Spider and the Fly,"* that Helpmann first saw Anna Pavlova. After that, Ballet, which until then had been merely a useful adjunct to an actor, beckoned.

Every night for eighteen months Helpmann watched Pavlova dancing. He travelled with the company over Australia and New Zealand taking lessons every day with Novikov. Every night he was in front watching. Then Margaret Rawlings, on tour in Australia, suggested that Helpmann should come to England and take lessons with "the girl who arranged the Dance of the Seven Veils for me in *Salome*. You know, Bobby," reflectively, "that girl's got something".

That girl has certainly given something. It is called The Sadler's Wells Ballet and has become our National Theatre of the Dance.

And so in 1932 Helpmann came to London and took lessons from Ninette de Valois. The Vic-Wells Ballet was then taking the first excited steps of its infancy. A toddle forward here. A catastrophe there. A picking up and a going on. And on.

In 1933 an international gathering of Economists was convened in London, in honour of which the Vic-Wells Ballet gave a gala performance at Covent Garden. The ballet chosen was *Coppélia*. In it, unforgettably, as guest artist, was Lopokhova. In it, also as guest artist, working furiously in the corps de ballet, was Robert Helpmann.

Coppélia over, and at the end of the series of lessons, a well-brushed Helpmann went to Sadler's Wells to say good-bye to Miss de Valois and to thank her for the terrific experience.

"See you next season"—pregnant pause—"here," she said. And legend has it that she added, "I can do something with that face." She did.

And so, a few months after he landed here, Helpmann found himself a member of the Vic-Wells Company, and hard work set in. It was work of the right kind to develop the brain of the artist as well as his line and limbs. He was working in a community, artistically segregated, led by Ninette de Valois, a woman of tremendous courage and a great distinction of mind. He was to work with Constant Lambert, a brilliant musician who, of his own free choice, has made Ballet his field, and did not land it in *faute-de-mieux*, and with a grudge against himself, his work, and fate. He

* Our hero was the Spider.

6

2. Helpmann as Comus

3. Gordon Hamilton as the Cuckoo in *The Birds*;
Moya Fraser as the Hen

was to work, too, with Frederick Ashton whose witty and sophisticated choreography he was to interpret for many years.

From the outset Helpmann worked for two excellent choreographers.

"How is it," I asked him once, "that your first ballet* is so complete? It seems to have been born grown up."

"That's because I've only worked for very good choreographers," he told me. "They always knew exactly what they wanted. And so do I."

I find this easy to believe of the man who created *Hamlet* in ten days on tour.

The first ballet in which Helpmann created the leading male rôle was *The Haunted Ballroom*, a Valois ballet to music by Geoffrey Toye, with décors by—daring innovation—the fashionable firm of stage designers who went by the name of Motley. Alicia Markova, ill suited but spiritual, was the ballerina.

For the next few years Robert Helpmann worked in the ballet, taking every rôle, suitable or unsuitable, that came his way, with eagerness and intelligence. And in those years certain outstanding qualities came generally to be recognised. Helpmann was always interested, and therefore interesting, when he was on the stage. His work was beginning to show a superb sense of line. (Not the turned-out line of limb that is the mark of the classical dancer; this, owing to his—balletically speaking—mis-spent youth, he has never achieved. But that feeling for line both in gesture and group that has now become so pleasing a content of his choreography.) Slowly he found a mastery, and later a virtuosity, in make-up. Years of dancing the classical rôles followed, first in alternation with Anton Dolin, and later, in succession to this superb cavalier, partnering Alicia Markova in his own right. Later still he was to partner first the budding and then the mature Margot Fonteyn.

This was the crowded progress that was to end in the creation of his own ballets. The years of unremitting work that have brought him their gift of authority. Years of work, and his natural elegance of mind.

No ballet was ever dull while Helpmann was on the stage. His characterisations became noticeable. Then deft. Then brilliantly comical. And with *The Rake* and *Hamlet*, deeply tragic. Though, for the present writer, at least, Helpmann has yet to prove that he is in touch with tears.

Camera studies of his ballets show clearly that his work as a choreographer mirrors those qualities that are to be found in his dancing. Study

* *Comus*.

plates 15 and 4 and see how the situation knots itself into dramatic groups. Note in plates 19 and 64 how line, both in the group and in the individual dancer, has been used. But no static photograph can quite convey the subtlety of his mime, or the wild certainty of his burlesque. Helpmann is a great *drôle*. To be peered, in his medium, only with Massine. But Massine gets his effects with a match-flare wit, while Helpmann builds his up from a labyrinth of richly comical detail.

II

"TEMPERAMENT," writes the distinguished critic James Agate in the best but four of the *Ego* books,* "is largely a matter of nationality." In other words, temperament is a matter of temperature—plus finance.

Nowhere can this be more readily perceived than in the English school of *Ballet Russe:* English because its temporal home is in London and because it has been created to please a British public by dancers who are British.

It will be interesting to see in which ways climate and mass environment will have conditioned the ballets created during this war by America for America. And later to note the American reaction to the Sadler's Wells Ballets when the company goes to the States, after the war.

For the arts derive their colour from the climate in which they are fostered, and are modified by it just as much as man's physical features and his palate.

Mass environment and the climate are responsible for, among other things, the music of Delius (who was driven by them to end his days abroad, but whose loveliest work, *Brigg Fair*, is as deeply and uncompromisingly national as anything by William Byrd or Vaughan Williams), the painting of Gainsborough, the plays of William Shakespeare, and the Ballet at Sadler's Wells.

Indeed, the Ballet in England might be held to be the Semite of the Arts, lavishing its alien qualities upon the startled land of its adoption. This does not mean that English Ballet is without its excellences, but that fundamentally it is conditioned by its differences.

The *Ballet Russe*, passing through Europe, has undergone certain changes. In Russia, during the decline of the Tsarist régime, composer and designer turned to folklore for inspiration. And so the sturdy, lively, coloured works of the Peasant Russian school were evolved—*Prince Igor*, *Petrouchka*, *Coq d'Or*, *L'Oiseau de Feu*, and many other works, as gay and bright as the colours of a back-cloth by Goncharova, as strong and exciting as a Gopak, and as durable as a fairy-tale.

But after the Russians went to Paris, *Ballet Russe* abandoned the sturdy for the intellectual; a sophistication of mind modified the greediness of the eye. Pushkin made way for Picasso. It was the day of Cocteau. It was the age of chi-chi.

Diaghilev died. Broadcasting began to beckon. The public, in England,

* *Ego 5*.

9

in America, and in Australia, became increasingly music-conscious. And so the symphonic ballet form was evolved. Tchaikovsky and, even less pardonably, Brahms, Bach, Beethoven and, as we shall see later, Berlioz, became choreographised. The dancer added an obbligato of movement to the orchestral scores. The choreographist attempted to pit his invention against musical development and manfully manœuvred his dancers into groups at the points of climax. Ballet-goers were split into two perennially articulate camps. Those (among whom the present writer must be numbered) who held that musical correspondences, as an end in themselves, made for bad ballet, worse music, and insufficient concentration upon either; contradicted by those who felt that to deny the choreo-symphony was to limit the scope of the art-form.

Later, however, Walt Disney, with his charming animated designs for the screen, pointed to the natural development of the visual accompaniment to the symphonic score. Eventually those who seek to see the work conceived in one art-form interpreted simultaneously in the terms of another will go to the cinema. Could anything be more suitable?

What did the English public demand of the creators of their Ballet? That, like the Russians, they should remember their traditions; should keep faith, as it were, with their roots. The English school of *Ballet Russe* is no Frenchified hybrid, but a sturdy growth that, in 1943, has withstood the test and drain of war.

If I were asked to name those Sadler's Wells creations which the company will be dancing fifty years from 1943 I would select one ballet by Ninette de Valois:

The Rake's Progress,

with possibly a second:

The Prospect Before Us.

Two works by Frederick Ashton:

Les Rendezvous,

Les Patineurs,

with possibly a third:

Apparitions.

And a work by Robert Helpmann:

Hamlet,

with possibly a second:

Comus.

I would, however, wish to make one important reservation—If the Sadler's Wells of posterity is to present *The Rake's Progress, Hamlet* and *Comus*, it will need to produce a dancer who is also an actor, just as the Sadler's Wells of 1942 trained, developed and sponsored Robert Helpmann.

10

4.   Balance, Line and Drama in a group from *Hamlet*

List Lady: be not coy and be not cozened

5. An interesting arrangement of line in *Comus*

III

FIRST let us consider the ballets by Frederick Ashton: *Les Rendezvous*, *Les Patineurs* and *Apparitions*.

Of the three choreographers who have lived and worked with the Sadler's Wells Company, Frederick Ashton's approach to his medium approximates the most closely to that of the Russians.

Ashton realises his situations in terms of the *pas* and the *enchainement*—the step and the sequence of steps. The world that he projects is intangible, to be imagined rather than to be perceived. His characterisation is achieved in shades of meaning and in subtleties.

I submit that had Ashton worked for an equal number of years with a Russian company away from English influences his idiom would have been enlarged to extend a brilliant and glittering cast, and his choreography would have taken on the strangeness of a Balanchine. As it is his wit has been harnessed to a more forthright utterance. Unlike the Americans, the English, in their Ballet as in their Literature, have no time for irony.

Les Rendezvous, to music by Auber, with a décor by William Chappell, is a charming work. It is deft. It is gay. It is subtle. It extends the dancer. It lifts the heart. It holds the quality of eternal surprise. And nowhere does it relinquish the interest.

The ballet is compounded of light and gaiety. In it, a radiant company is engagingly met. Its event and characterisation are like the colours in a bubble, or the wind-made ripples on a lake. Its solo variations are deft. It has a *pas de trois* that is a model of its kind—gay, evocative and witty. And, as always in his work, Ashton's lifts, by their timing, their line and their intention, are superb and lend the work something of their own *ballon*.

As it happens *Les Rendezvous* has its Russian counterpart: *Cotillon*, to music by Chabrier, with décors by Christian Bérard.

Here we have another radiant gathering. But the event of this ballet is strange and wild—always sophisticated and sometimes sinister. Both ballets have dancing sequences of abiding interest. Both are the best in their kind. But *Les Rendezvous* has the freshness, in its frolics, of a new cake of soap. *Cotillon* is built upon a rising excitement. The difference here is a national difference—a veritable field-day triumph of temperature over temperament.

Les Patineurs, to music by Meyerbeer, with décor by William Chappell, is another altogether delightful ballet. Ashton has turned his stage into a Victorian ice-rink, and his cast into skaters—over-balanced beginners and whizzing experts, enchantingly dressed. The humours of the work are sturdy, and, for *Ballet Russe*, slap-stick. Ashton, by using familiar classical *pas* in a new context, has given them a different shade of meaning.

Massine, in a like situation, would have brought a wealth of invention to the choreography. Cruikshank would have peopled his rink with busy tingling characters which the choreographer would have treated with a French simplification.

Les Patineurs, considered choreographically, is a charming and interesting work, well timed and nicely knit together. Like *Les Rendezvous*, it is a work for dancers rather than for a star-personality (save for the rôle of Male Expert, which has not been adequately danced since Harold Turner, for whom it was created, left the company). And, like the latter, the dancers are to be seen at their best in it. Where individual virtuosity is called for in this ballet, as in *Les Rendezvous*, it is invariably produced by the company for whom it was devised.

At the time of writing it suffers from being put on as a first ballet, without principals and without snow. It is to be hoped that posterity will not be suffering from a paper shortage.*

It is to be hoped, too, that posterity will use *Les Patineurs* as a last ballet, sending audiences out into the bright lights while the movement and gaiety is still in their minds. "Those were the days" posterity will murmur indulgently, almost enviously, queueing up for the last plane home.

Apparitions is a ballet in the romantic manner. The story of the Poet and his Inspiration. A very English Poet found dreaming in the library at Knole of a very English Inspiration for all the Italianate funeral rites, and all ending in an ever so English orgy, though it has to be conceded that the home team wear the same colours as the visitors.†

But there are charming passages in the work, notably the scene at the ball with its elegant and, as dressed by Cecil Beaton, exquisite revellers. And Constant Lambert's presentation of Liszt has a great romantic sweep, so that somehow I think that while the company continues to produce

* That is what this one is strictly in aid of.   † Slack, Mr. Beaton!

dancers who can act, they will continue to give this romantic ballet, debility, drugs, débutantes, decontamination squads and all.

Apparitions has a direct Russian counterpart—*Symphonie Fantastique*, the Massine ballet to music by Berlioz with décors by Christian Bérard.

Here, more or less as laid down in the programme of the music, is the Poet, his Potion, his *bien-aimée*, and his lithe hornèd devils. A Mass of the Damned, a strongly inventive Judgment scene, and a most poetic picnic. Here, too, no richness has been spared. Compared to the Bérard conception, Beaton can be likened to an elegant Laurencin, set beside a sturdy Rubens. Bérard's scarlet ballroom swept fitfully with black and white dancers, and the noble aqueduct with which he furnishes forth the al fresco junketings have charged the ballet with atmosphere, and perfectly express the rich, fierce and often comical score.

Massine applies his symphonic manner to the telling of his tale. In the Potion scene the Poet is surrounded by his fancies—units of the absolute in lengths of coloured tulle. But in the ballroom the choreographer discards the musical correspondence and the involved group, affixed to the stage in a quivering kind of *collage*, for a more accustomed arrangement of sweeping *entrées*, swaying and billowing across the stage against the heightened sinister scarlet set.

The al fresco scene sees a return to musical correspondences and in its earlier presentation Massine flew *la bien-aimée* over the ruined aqueduct, hoist, no doubt, on her own petard. (It is a sobering thought that in our time we shall not see the broken aqueduct, nor indeed any other form of romantic ruin, without the instant reaction "Bomb damage". And when the feathered dancers, the four winds, look up at the sky as the motif of *la bien-aimée* is sounded, we shall think of our roof-spotting days or remember camouflage.)

But in the Judgment scene Massine forsakes the symphonic and reverts to the inventive—that invention of which he is the greatest exponent that the Ballet has yet known. After the stylised torture and terror of the Judgment, Hell is a bitter disappointment. The Forces of Darkness cannot be expressed in terms of the *fouetté*, however triumphant, nor even by covering the stage with a crawling corps, as it were, de belly.

But even if Hell, as a conception, is unattainable in an animated pictorial form, the work has a richness, an atmosphere, and an emotional impact that is lacking in its English counterpart.

The obvious explanation is that Ashton-Lambert-Beaton were never after impact, but instead preferred the literary romanticism born of reading

Dante late at night in the Library at Knole—a Kentish midsummer's night's dream, not a Bavarian Walpurgis. Surely here we have a clear example of the complete triumph of environment over art-form. Accentuated a little by a tight purse.

Before leaving the work of Ashton it is interesting to note that he has been the first choreographer to use direct quotation in his ballets with full literary intention. In the filial Stravinsky ballet, *Baiser de la Fée*, he quotes Petipa, in a gesture of homage. And in his later *Harlequin in the Street* he quotes, wickedly and unmistakably, the exit of the lovers in Massine's great *pas-de-deux* in *Les Présages*—a memorable passage in an otherwise pretentious work.

IV

NINETTE DE VALOIS has a double claim to the gratitude of the ballet-goer.
A dancer turned choreographist, she has founded, fostered, directed and
held together the Sadler's Wells Company. Like Ashton she has worked
closely with the Russians. But her approach to choreography is governed
less by nuance and subtlety—more by forthright statement. And often, it
must be admitted, by downright reiteration.

Of the three choreographers at present under discussion, Valois is the
least musical, the most pictorial. In her work repetition is frequently to be
found where a theme in the music is repeated or re-stated. It is as though
she accepts the ordered passages of sound as a necessary adjunct to movement in ballet, but is neither challenged nor inspired by it to further
invention after a first successful statement.

But she can animate a background with a completeness and assurance
that is without rival.

Valois is moved to subtleties and deft characterisations by a feeling
for the period which she is projecting. She has a great instinct for the past.
No designer could ask for a more ingenious collaborator.

The best work of this choreographist in the Wells repertory—one would
be tempted to acclaim it the best work of any modern choreographer
presented by this company but for Fokine's *Les Sylphides* and Helpmann's
Hamlet—is *The Rake's Progress*, to music by Gavin Gordon with a décor by
Rex Whistler after Hogarth.

Here choreographist, composer and designer are of one mind, and
their work interlocks admirably. The designer reflects Hogarth. The
composer reflects and indeed quotes from music of the period. And the
choreographist animates the pictures from the past. *The Rake's Progress* is a
poignant work. It is also richly comical. But, like all the best comedy, its
laughter is balanced on a tear. And being a Valois ballet, it has wit, movement and atmosphere—in short it is brimming over with life seen by a
keen and an amused beholder. Like life it has its irrelevances. But the
choreographist shares with the Russians the gift of imparting to the dancer
a world of meaning, faintly but gaily perceived.

The Rake, as danced by Robert Helpmann, sets out with all the pathos
of a young kitten. He savours his sudden fortune with eagerness and with
wonder. He learns to flout his tailor. He is instructed in the art of the
dance and is lost in marvel at his own graceful fingers. He is fascinated by
the French horn. Stay, he has even Betrayed a Pure Young Maid. He soon
finds his way to a brothel. This is a fine bawdy scene, strongly characterised

and full of, to the writer, unexpected event. Next he takes to the dice. Here tremendous excitement infuses the comedy. The excitement of the gamblers, waiting for the Rake. And the ghastly fever of the consistent and now despairing loser.

The last sad scene is the asylum. Poor crazed creature, almost too pitiful to be comical, the green, wild, twitching madness of the Rake shot through with terror at his end. This scene is just bearable for the feeling of inevitability with which it is charged and because of the response it finds in the pity of the audience.

The present writer has no doubt at all that this ballet will be given in fifty years' time, if the company at that date can produce a dancer who can act. Possibly he will be less elegant than Robert Helpmann. Possibly less dazzlingly virtuistic. Almost certainly less volatile. But so long as there is an English school of ballet, capable of producing its own artistes, and of attracting its own public, like *Giselle* and *Les Sylphides*, *The Rake's Progress* will be performed. It goes right back to our past and in it is enshrined a part of our tradition.

The second Valois ballet suggested, more tentatively, for our Jubilee, is *The Prospect Before Us*, to music by Boyce arranged by Constant Lambert, with designs by Roger Furse after Rowlandson.

This is a witty, evocative work, with a great deal of subtle characterisation and lashings of slap-stick to gladden the heart. Is it a trifle over-lavish with its episodes, over-ample in its parodied ballet section, over-crowded in its animation, repetitive in its continuity sections? Possibly posterity will cut it here and there. Possibly Miss de Valois will spare them this embarrassing necessity. For the work has vitality, observation and gusto. It has tremendous charm. And in its tipsy Irishman, a creation in the *genre* that Massine has made his own, and which only that master of the subtle-burlesque could equal. But whereas Massine brings pathos to his sorties into the burlesque—a can-can dancer who is a dapper denizen of a lost world, a Peruvian, clearly everybody's orphan, a bar-tender fit to break the heart —Robert Helpmann gives the staggering impish little man a gaiety that is wholly enchanting and which makes him a memorable creation in a gallery of memorable creations.

Indeed, taking it by and much too large, rid *The Prospect Before Us* of its redundancies, and a masterly animation of the past will be found to have emerged. It has been suggested that Miss de Valois should create a Dickens Ballet. I hope quite fervently that this work is already under way—to a décor after Cruikshank with music by the composer of *Pop Goes the Weasel!*

V

ROBERT HELPMANN, dancer and choreographer, has, more than any dancer of his day, with the exception of Massine, influenced the ballet of our time.

Massine, virtuoso stylist, brings a wealth of subtle invention and a quality of great pathos to the ballets in which he dances. Other choreographers have been less successful for him—or he with them. Robert Helpmann, a dancer of elegance rather than technical brilliance, by reason of his quite singular sense of the theatre, has modified the ballet in this country. Vehicles have had to be devised to extend his virtuosity, and to frame his special qualities of drama and comedy. And the artist who has emerged from all this has been crowned by his own *Hamlet*.

Let us recall some of his work as a dancer before passing to his choreography, for those qualities which have distinguished his dancing are reflected, sure pointers, in his choreography. For the choreographer takes to his creations those qualities that he brings to his interpretive characterisations. A work by Massine will have a lithe quickness, sophistication and pity. A Valois ballet will have wit, strength and on occasion a pointedness that is quite shattering. And Helpmann's ballets are dramatic, musical, elegant, adult and set forth in impeccable line—that faultless line from wrist to shoulder that is so true a grace in his dancing.

First we can manage to descry him in that most imperceptible of all rôles the ballet has to offer—the Nut-Cracker in the *divertissement* act of *Casse Noisette*. This is no small feat, for the male dancer, here, is little more than the tinselled and elegant stay to the radiant ballerina. Even the variations he is called upon to do are well-bred to the point of nullity, and leave as much impress upon the ballet as a smile that has died from the face of a diplomat.

Helpmann subdues his personality to a helpful blank. A faintly felt device for supporting the ballerina with masterly timing and superb *port de bras*, the very nearly invisible personification of tact. Indeed, line, timing (by which I mean a feeling for the musical phrase as well as the precise split second at which to throw out an arm, extend a palm, raise a head—those qualities for which Arnold Haskell has coined the unpleasing word "musicality" but which in these pages will be known as "timing"),

17

tact, style, and a quality that comes from a natural elegance of mind, which, for want of a better word, I will call authority, are the motivating influences in Helpmann's work, both as dancer and as choreographer.

Recall his adroit handling of melancholy as The Prince in *The Sleeping Princess*, and remember how remote is laughter from us, even when, worried and dressed in green, he cannot conceive how to waken the Princess and has to be egged on thereto by the Lilac Fairy, and even though Tchaikovsky clinches the encounter with a smart blow on the cymbals. Harps are more usually the accompaniment to Love's Awakening. Silence, though tricky, would probably be more effective than either. Earlier in the same ballet Helpmann portrays a most satisfying evil hag, the fairy Carrabose, with the brilliantly imaginative make-up which is so much a feature of his work.

Think of his pale poet in *Apparitions*, and how, with so little to help him in the expense of money, so much in the squandering of imagination, deftly and definitely, he wrings our heart. We share his elation when he leaves the ball, going over, in his mind, the paces of the dance he joined with the Beloved One. We suffer his tension at the dread purple *funérailles*. Our heart breaks with his, when he can no longer support his life. Indeed, we share at the very opening of the ballet his headache when he cannot find a new rhyme to June and so takes to drugs. If he had had a rhyming dictionary there might have been no ballet . . .

A finely sustained study in dishevelled romanticism.

Giselle, every dancer's dream, still eludes Helpmann. He lacks the fire of Dolin in the rôle and the inspired conceit of Lifar. He cannot convince the present writer by his performance, though it must be admitted that to the question "Who else could dance it in this company?" there can be only one answer: "Who, indeed?"

As the Prince in *Lac des Cygnes* Helpmann is happier. Though it seems to the writer—partly because he lacks the pure classical turned-out line—that he is far from being a model in the classics.

Dancers could be divided into four clear categories:

1. Those born to appear in *Giselle* and *Lac des Cygnes*.
2. Those born to dance *Petrouchka*.
3. Those born to beat, leap and flout the pull of the earth.
4. Massine.

In assessing the work of Robert Helpmann it is necessary to note one important factor. To the foregoing classification he has added a fifth:

18

6. Helpmann as Hamlet

No more, sweet Hamlet!

7. Robert Helpmann and Celia Franca

5. Those born to be Hamlet and old Coppelius. And to indulge his public by never making a fool of himself in any rôle in between.

Moreover, like Massine, Helpmann is destined to write his own classics. Vehicles that will discover heart and later perhaps even simplicity in their creator.

The writer is now to embark on what may well prove to be the longest parenthesis known to recorded time outside of the learned works of Krafft-Ebing. It concerns the Fokine ballet *Carnaval*. I have seen the poet, Eusebius, perfectly portrayed by two artistes—Massine and Woizikowsky. Dolin has too brightly hopeful a personality for Eusebius. Dancers of a lesser artistic stature diminish the rôle. The writer takes this opportunity to challenge Mr. Helpmann to this rôle. She will not even take mean advantage of the harp box, but will remain a happy blob in the front row of the dress circle. Early in his career Mr. Helpmann danced the Poet—the only thoroughly bad performance the writer has seen him give. This was before Mr. Helpmann had made acquaintance with dignity, and was relying upon hope and a high degree of courage, these qualities being, after all, those that make the accomplished dancer in the end.

In the days when Mr. Helpmann was so notably courageous the company was giving *Carnaval* as a first ballet at every press night.* These performances were remarkable for two things: the virtuoso dancing of Harold Turner as Harlequin, the only completely satisfying exponent of the rôle since Idzikowsky. And, taking the Ballet as a whole, a valuable indication of what the Sadler's Wells public would forgive and applaud. Lately this ballet has lapsed from the repertory.

I suggest that it be revived and used to replace the over-immaculate *Sylphides* which the company is at present perpetrating.

The company, at its present artistic strength, could give a very good account of itself in this Fokine *Rendezvous*. And forthwith I propose to append a cast:

Eusebius, the Poet: Robert Helpmann.

(Mr. Helpmann owes us this reparation, and we owe the opportunity of making it to him.)

Chiarina: {Beryl Grey
                               {Celia Franca

* The fact that it couldn't matter less if you missed it must have heartened many of my delayed colleagues.

19

The rôle calls for an exponent of generous personality. One who can perceive the poetry of the *adages* in the *pas de trois*.

Grey has the sparkling radiant generosity of youth—Franca a more mature, more smooth expanse of spirit.

| *Papillon:* | Margaret Dale |
| | Joan Sheldon |

Margaret Dale is a young dancer of great integrity, whose appearance on the stage—one might almost call it a taking of the stage—is always a focus of attention.

Joan Sheldon, though she lacks the personality of the true ballerina, has a pleasing lightness, pace and line, and answers well to the demands that are made upon her.

Pierrot: Alexis Rassine.

Rassine is a young dancer of the first promise. Lithe and graceful, he can be relied upon always to give a performance. At his present stage of technical development it is sometimes a bad performance. But Rassine does not spare himself, and though it is doubtful if he will ever be a reliable cavalier to the ballerina, I am confident that here we have a variation soloist who could go to the Russians and hold his own among them.

Harlequin: Gordon Hamilton.

Gordon Hamilton might be adequate now and later a distinguished Harlequin.

Columbine:

Well, here we have the chief difficulty in casting this ballet for the Wells.

The rôle calls for a more stylised treatment than Margot Fonteyn, with the gift of taking simplicity, the more touching for the layer of sophistication that it has recently acquired, is wont to permit herself.

Julia Farron, the little lost girl of the Ballet, might be rather too self-consciously arch. It is outside anything that Margaret Dale has yet attempted. Would Jean Bedells—smooth and dependable—be a little too china-doll-like?

Confronted with this delicate piece of casting, the Parenthesist gracefully passes the ballerina to Miss de Valois. Her choice shall be our choice, so long as Mr. Helpmann appears as Eusebius on press nights.

And now to return to Robert Helpmann's present excellences.

Foremost among these is his richly comical Doctor Coppelius in the ballet *Coppélia*.

Here Helpmann has taken the fustian doll-maker and touched him to veritable life—an ancient creased and rheumy life, impish at its ebb, vitalised by spite, warmed by rage—a cranky, creviced, spell-spun life, which has been lying in the old work waiting for Helpmann to discover it. For he has given the toy-maker a swift crabby hobble. A crusty rage. And an unplumbed world of snuffy evilness. Helpmann's Pygmalion is wildly comical. He is the living manifestation of Gothic impishness. And incidentally this is one of Helpmann's masterpieces of make-up.

But in the dark shadows of the room where the mechanical toys beam and have their jerky movement, and the doll-like ballerina goes through her stiff paces, Helpmann loses touch with pathos. There is nothing in his wild inventive and rich performance for tears. Not for a second does this old toy-maker droop into a white weariness that has taken a life-time of activity to gather. You cannot feel sorry for him. So that when the curtain falls on a tableau of his despair at finding his magic doll was just a mortal, you know that this Coppelius would never have collapsed and torn his hair, but sat up, run his fingers through his frizz, and babbled of green fields.

"A ballet without an audience is like a cherry orchard without the cherry trees." And I suppose the ballet-goer is the most responsive audience known to man.* And the audience takes a very real part in every performance. And how the war-time audiences at the New Theatre revel in Robert Helpmann revelling in Coppelius.

The Prospect Before Us presents Helpmann with the gayest of his creations. The fey little Irishman who, in the hands of a lesser actor would pass for an amusing secondary character, has been built up by Helpmann with a thousand deft touches of observation and instinct. Once again his virtuosity in make-up plays a major part in his realisation of the rôle. And in the tipsy travesty of the ballerina's dance Helpmann has created a characterisation that ranks with Massine's bar-man in *Union Pacific* and with the little Peruvian Traveller in his *Gaîté Parisienne*.

* In war-time, however, the ballet-goer is a bad second to a man on a cliff watching a flight of Spitfires. But if the man on the cliff combines both functions he will argue that a flight of Spits have a balletic line.

VI

AND now we come to Helpmann's choreography. Let us examine it for the traces of those gifts that have made him one of the leading dancers of his day. His sense of situation expressed in line. His great gift of drollery. His singular—almost uncanny—sense of characterisation.

From the outset Helpmann's work shows intellectual grasp and a masterly treatment of technical difficulties.

Drama, expressed in exquisite line, is Helpmann's *forte*. His groups fall naturally and dramatically into the punctuation of his story, like the chords of a Beethoven Symphony. And, like all good groups, each conveys a concerted comment on the progress of the situation.

Comus was Helpmann's first ballet.* It was a very daring project for a new choreographer. The narrative of the Masque has joins in it which fall awkwardly for the choreographer, and it has to be admitted that these joins have defeated Helpmann. Mr. Messel, who has designed the distinguished and very beautiful décor, has been unhelpful here. Possibly, once again, it has been a matter of those purse-strings which seem to divide our national Ballet so sharply from the fashionable *Ballet Russe*.

But I submit that an arrangement of gauzes would provide a more effective screen and cause less of a break in that perilous asset, mood, than bringing down the house curtains on Part One, and that with light and gauzes floating and lifting a more lucent dawning could be effected than the finalities of the black-out before the rising of Sabrina.

Two such uncompromising breaks in one short ballet must be admitted to be flaws unless those breaks can be woven more cunningly into the texture of the narrative.

The rising of Sabrina paying out mazes of blue chiffon has been much discussed. Personally I like the conception. I have a quaint old-fashioned preference for beauty of movement, design and light in ballet, and shimmering blue Sabrina, gracefully attended, fulfils this fancy of mine.

But the most striking innovation in this first work of a new choreographer is his treatment of Comus—a rôle which he takes himself.

Comus speaks. And the sky remains above us! He speaks Milton's lines from the stage. And speaks them beautifully.

* Helpmann devised a modest chamber-ballet, *La Danse*, for a single performance at the Cambridge Theatre, in May 1939, but this stands in relation to his mature work as a Bagatelle to the finished Sonata.

8. Helpmann as Comus

9. Break off, break off! I feel the different pace
   Of some chaste footing near about this ground.

10.   Helpmann as Comus

11. Come, knit hands and beat the ground.

12. 'Tis only daylight that makes sin.

Here indeed is an innovation. And, incidentally, one that must not be encouraged into a bent.*

Words have been sung in ballets, and spoken through microphones in the orchestra pit. But in *Comus*, the dancer, the centre of an arrested group of "Ounce or tiger, hog or bearded goat", speaks from the stage.

Then, again, the music, which, with its classical form and repetition, far from being the "sound of riot and ill-managed merriment, such as the joconde flute or gamesome pipe stirs up among the loose unlettered hinds", lacks the flow and freedom of a swift story-telling element, such as the Tchaikovsky music in *Hamlet* or the Stravinsky music for *Petrouchka*.

Moreover, and with his eyes open, this new choreographer has let himself in for an orgy. Now Helpmann must know, just as well as the present writer, that orgies in ballets somehow never quite contrive to jell. And not even Massine can infuse an element of electricity into a Bacchanalia. But in spite of measured movement and immovable mask the choreographer has devised a very telling "wavering morrice to the moon". And Mr. Messel's masks, though they prove less hindrance than most (for the dancer, with no voice to convey emotion, has a greater need than any type of actor for the freedom of at least a part of his face), rob the dancer of his climaxes of horror. The artist has the sanction of Milton's text. Moreover, it is doubtful whether head-dresses and half-masks would serve the subject half so well as Mr. Messel's permanent pussyfaces. Goncharova, faced with much the same problem in *L'Oiseau de Feu*, solved it in much the same way. And Mr. Messel more than makes up for the unchanging countenances of the rout of monsters, by the back-cloth for Act One with its illimitable vistas of sylvan joyances, his noble table set against the grey grotto of Act Two, Circe's ruby goblet, and the infinitely evil scarlet of Comus's apparel.

It will be seen, then, that for his first ballet Helpmann chose no simple little vehicle which he could animate without doing anyone very much harm or himself very much good. He chose to try his strength against a major subject, the difficulties of which could be neither glossed over nor concealed. In choosing this subject he showed himself to be both wise and courageous. For the drama, the colour and the originality of the treatment masked his meagre vocabulary of the recognised classical *enchainement*.

This meagreness of vocabulary must, I think, have been his greatest

* The writer is obsessed by a vista of ballerinas, all with the light voices of dancers (for however heavy-footed a dancer may be her voice is always surprisingly light—even when it is low in pitch), declaiming at least Greek tragedy.

concern in his first ballet. For already he knew himself to be a master of stage situation. But, like the clever artist that he is, he turned his technical shortcomings to good account and contrived to make his defects serve his ends, and with great skill in inventiveness, and even greater skill in characterisation, he proceeded to master his problems. He has "adapted" his subject with freedom and certainty, so that, though it springs from a literary source, its treatment is never "literary". *Comus*, in fact, might have been conceived in the first place as a drama of movement. Certainly it achieves an effective statement in movement, without recourse to written words, though those that are spoken add to the intensity with which the Masque is enacted.

Not since Fokine has there been a choreographer with so sure a claim on our sincerity as Robert Helpmann. Suffering Hamlet. The Lost Lady in *Comus*. The radiant Nightingale. All these touch us with their emotions, even as the earlier ballet-goer was moved to suffer with Petrouchka, and to tremble with the Princess in her charmed encounter with the Prince in *L'Oiseau de Feu*.

Massine, too, can charm us to a tear with his choreography, as in *Boutique Fantasque*, when the doll is borne away from the shop on the shoulders of her companions, and with the grieving *entrée* of the faithful wife in *Femmes de Bonne Humeur*. But Massine's approach to our emotions is far more complex. He makes us weep for the moment, keenly sensed, that will not come again—a moment composed partly of mood, partly of music and light and movement. And if we were asked why we wept we could not clearly say. A complicated alchemy in which timing and intention and perhaps accident play each a part.

Helpmann's claim on our emotion comes from the drama, the strength and the poignancy of the story he has to tell, and is a direct statement in stagecraft. In *Comus* the story is swift and dramatic. A Lady, journeying to her parents, becomes separated from her two brothers and lost in an awesome wood. She meets Comus, disguised as a shepherd, who leads her to his haunt. There he throws off his meek disguise and tries to dazzle and tempt her to drink the cordial julep from his charmed goblet which will change her into a creature with a woman's body but the head of a beast. The Attendant Spirit, however, has the Lady in her charge and leads her brothers to the nightmare orgy where they overpower Comus and his rout and deliver their sister, unharmed.

It will be seen that the fable follows Milton's text as closely as an effective transposition into another medium allows.

From the outset Helpmann's claim on our emotions is established.

The Lady, lost in the "perplexed paths of the ominous wood", has a poignant simplicity that brings its terrors close to the heart.

24

Why should you be so cruel to yourself
And to those dainty limbs, which Nature meant
For gentle usage and soft delicacy?

13.   Robert Helpmann and Margot Fonteyn

14. The star that bids the shepherd fold
Now the top of heaven doth hold.

15.   Strict age and sour severity
With their grave saws in slumber lie,
We that are of purer fire
Imitate the starry quire.

Due west it rises from this shrubby point.

16. Robert Helpmann and Margot Fonteyn

Much like his father, but his mother more.

17. Robert Helpmann as Circe's son

Can any mortal mixture of earth's mould
Breathe such divine enchanting ravishment?
18.   Robert Helpmann and Margot Fonteyn

Thyrsis lead on apace, I'll follow thee—
And some good angel bear a shield before us

19.   A study in line from *Comus*

20.   Pas de Deux, *Comus*

21. Helpmann as Comus

From these gates
Sorrow flies far.

22.   Robert Helpmann and Margot Fonteyn

And first behold this cordial julep here
That flames and dances in his crystal bounds.

23.   Robert Helpmann as Comus

None but such as are good men can give good things.

24. Robert Helpmann and Margot Fonteyn

25.   A group from *Comus*

26.   Virtue Triumphant

> "This way the noise was, if mine ear be true,
> My best guide now."

The rôle is fortunate in its two protagonists—Margot Fonteyn with her smooth brilliancy, and Beryl Grey with the radiance and pathos of still being very young.

But before the *entrée* of the Lady there have been two important characterisations: the Attendant Spirit, dressed in her sky-robes, spun out of Iris's woof. And Comus, ivy-crowned, bearing the charmèd cup from which "whoever tasted lost his upright shape and downwards fell into a grovelling swine".

The choreography for the Nymph is strong, vengeful and sexless, the characterisation springing, as it were, from her long pointed eyebrows, from the pointing fingers and from the flailing arms. The Spirit does in fact bestride the glade like a minuscule Colossus, the living embodiment of the lashing whip that later she wields.

The demands made upon the dancer, technically and artistically, are considerable. Vera Nemchinova, at the height of her technical perfection, could have danced this rôle as it needs to be danced. The present writer can think of no other dancer with the same strength, precision and sexlessness.

Comus is a rôle devised by the choreographer for himself. And like so many of Helpmann's rôles, the contents of his make-up box have become an integral part of the rôle, and as much an element of the ballet as Milton's speeches and the movements in which the story is conveyed. This does not mean that Mr. Helpmann is content to rely upon his make-up for the projection of his rôles. No one seeing him in *The Rake's Progress*, from the eager impatience of youth through its decay into a green and twitching madness, could doubt that here is an actor.

Comus is less sinister than elegant—a graceful youth in love with sin. So must Circe's son have been. He could have been no other. Comus follows his dark gods readily and plausibly—Milton has seen to that—and his tragedy, to an extent, becomes our own. The forces that created him move to no other end.

Indeed, there is a great deal of Pan about the son of Bacchus, a swiftness of movement and a compelling persuasiveness, and there is something of most of us in his final discomfiture—an effective figure, simple in statement and certain in his unwitting appeal to our charity.

Mime and movement have served the Lady well, taking from her the priggishness of "the virtuous mind that ever walks attended by a strong siding champion, Conscience", of which she prates. And silence emphasises the pathos and fragility of the little lost Creature.

She dances on the *pointes*, as do the Attendant Spirit and Sabrina. And though this is strictly out of period, it lends her an added fragility and is, I think, artistically the right treatment for the feminine element in a fable, and for Spirits and Goddesses.

And the scoring for the Lady is economical and effective. The choreographer has drawn her with direct and simple movements, conceived always in terms of the situation and the progress of events. There is no digression into the extended variation or the virtuistic *pas-de-deux*. Movement is subordinate always to the progress of the plot, and the story holds our attention and kindles our imagination because it is never held up for some balletic *tour de force*. Action, mood and choreography move forward together, the inalienable voices in the choreographic score.

To perfunctory modern ears, the two Lordlings, too, are better company in dumb play than in the uncut passages of the book, their prosiness transmuted into energetic and elegant movement. Indeed, their double *entrée* is one of the most distinctive things in the ballet (Plate 20). Danced with an adroitness which the company cannot at the moment provide, their *entrée* in Act 1 would show itself to be an effective essay in line, economy and precision.

Sabrina's attended *entrée*, in Act 2, has some pleasant weaving movement, amid a haze of what, in *Green Pastures*, is always alluded to as "Firmament". And this important figure artfully removes the ending of the ballet from the slightly perfunctory.

Indeed, it is difficult to realise that this strongly knit ballet is a first work. It has all the omissions of a practised hand, and the innovations are those of a mature practitioner.

And though the text has been (I submit quite rightly) treated freely in its transposition from one art-form to another, the spirit of the text has been carefully, indeed tenderly, preserved. The wood in which the action of the Masque takes place is quite recognisably threaded with "perplexèd paths, the nodding horror of whose shady brows threats the forlorn and

27.   Virtue may be assailed, but never hurt.

Why are you vexed, Lady, why do you frown?

28. Robert Helpmann and Margot Fonteyn

29. Sabrina fair, attended.

30. Vice Discomfited: another study of line from *Comus*

wondering passenger". The table in the Grotto is duly set with "all manner of deliciousness"—or we could swear that this was so! And of the Lady we feel with Comus "sure something holy (or simple, defenceless, but with a flame of courage, gently expressed) lodges in that breast". And the Spirit might well—indeed, must—dwell "before the starry threshold of Jove's Court". Comus is "ripe and frolic of his full-grown age" and one can well believe that, his orient liquor in a crystal glass, and with Mr. Helpmann's personal magnetism, he excels his mother at her mighty arts. And as for Sabrina, she has emerged from a most authentic "glassy, cool, translucent wave"—"Goddess of a silver lake," who clearly keeps her band-box in cold storage.

The groupings in this work are effortless and effective. The stage picture is always presented with an ineffable sense of line (Plates 30 and 23) and with a balanced nobility of disposition (Plate 26), at all times effective and at some times beautiful. Those qualities that give enduring pleasure in a ballet are to be found here in abundance, even though there is no dancing interest of the through-the-hoop and over-the-hurdle school. But there remain the abiding pleasures of good line, deft characterisation, simplicity of treatment and unviolated mood.

A notable early work by a man with a great instinct for Theatre.

VII

HELPMANN's second ballet, *Hamlet*, has raised a storm of controversy. The ballet was heralded by the heaviest doubts.

What could Helpmann add to Shakespeare?

How would Hurry—newest of all "new" artists—combine with Tchaikovsky, and both with the philosophy and feeling of Shakespeare?

The ballet-goer was, in prospect, definitely shaken. So, incidentally, was the Good Shakespearean.

But Helpmann, with the discretion that has moulded all his seasoned work, has set his ballet in the split-second after Shakespeare's play is ended, taking for his theme the line: "For in that sleep of death what dreams may come?"

The action lies during the bearing of Hamlet's body from the stage, the curtain of the ballet rising on the picture of horror that is the play's ending, with Hamlet being borne off by Fortinbras' four Captains. The curtain of the ballet falls upon a reprise of that same heavy sight, the rondo of remembered action being logically and dreadfully completed. So that Helpmann's dissolving nightmare fulfils the function of a Freudian footnote to Shakespeare's text.

As a ballet, *Hamlet* is strongly dramatic. Again the dancing interest is subservient to that of the story. And Helpmann has given it the fluent treatment of the film. The lingering tale of indecision becomes a drama of dreadful action in Hamlet's racing recollection.

Helpmann, Hurry and Tchaikovsky combine to make *Hamlet* the most fluent and smoothest ballet that the present writer has ever seen.

Hamlet is Helpmann's favourite rôle. His whole style is suited to its pace and fitfulness. In fact, I should think that if anyone were to put it to him, Helpmann would agree that he was born to dance Hamlet, just as Massine was born to dance the Miller in *Le Tricorne*.

For he brings to the rôle a nervous intensity and a sincerity, both in the choreography and in the interpretation of the rôle, that he, alone of all dancers, can best bestow upon it.

Just as Massine, in addition to being a superb stylist, brings an impishness and a great pathos to the rôles that he devises for himself, so Robert Helpmann brings pace, elegance, a lovely line of arm and shoulder, faultless timing and an unerring sense of the dramatic (all qualities to be found in his work as an interpreter of other choreographers' creations) to his own choreography.

Some day perhaps the sincerity that he brings to his own creations will lead him to the gift of tears.

The story of *Hamlet*, as balleticised, lies in the agonised timelessness of Hamlet's final exit.

As the livid light fades on the scene of death the ballet begins to flow. The Gravedigger, wearing the skull of Yorick, first of the ballet's significant duplications, scampers across, and Hamlet, touched with the weariness of death (which is the gathered weariness of life), descends to the empty stage (Plates 31-34).

There are a number of significant duplications in the ballet, the first of which is this Gravedigger-Yorick fusion, which is a natural and simple merging of two characters. Hamlet, about to die, recalls two certainties of death from his recent experience. The Gravedigger. And his recent shock at seeing the skull of Yorick. The pace of the recollection merges these two images, so that in the speed of the dream they are indivisible.

The image of the Gravedigger slides away and is replaced by the image of his father's ghost: "Hamlet, remember me!" He is accoutred as for battle:

> "Such was the very armour he had on
> When he th'ambitious Norway combated."*
>
> (Plate 35.)

The Ghost glides away. The stage lights up. And now image after image beats mercilessly up in Hamlet's brain. The Queen, his mother, wearing her beauty like a banner. Ophelia, his love. They waver and fade and replace one another and bloom afresh before him. He makes to hold one and finds that he is clutching the other.

This is the most important duplication in the ballet, and is echoed and re-echoed in a complicated series through the racing dream.

Ophelia takes leave of her brother Laertes in a kittenish *pas-de-deux*, and turns straight away to Hamlet, while the King and her father watch the lovers, hidden. Hamlet discovers the eavesdroppers and turns furiously upon Ophelia.

"God has given you one face and you make yourselves another: you jig, you amble and you lisp, and nickname God's creatures . . . to a Nunnery, go!"

Another image beats up in Hamlet's brain. The Play. With the Queen glowing out to her new husband. The curious courtiers gathered to witness

* I shall have something to say of this aspect of the Ghost at a later stage.

the Rat-Trap. The small page pointing to Hamlet and jeering at his distraught behaviour.

The play within the play has its significant duplications. Ophelia becomes the Player-Queen. The Ghost becomes the Player-King. They enact the poison scene in the orchard.

The image dissolves and now other images come beating up. The King-Uncle at prayer in his closet. The Queen. Polonius, killed behind the arras:

"Thou wretched, rash, intruding fool, farewell,
I took thee for thy better."

And now Ophelia again! "Stark mad in white satin," or, to be exact, white marguerites—the heralds of much madness in the annals of Ballet.*

And now the last horror-filled duplications take place. Drowned Ophelia becomes the Queen. And the Ophelia-Player Queen, wearing her river (it streams in sky-blue folds from the spikes of her Pinchbeck crown to the tips of her green-shod feet [Plate 48], so that she is, quite veritably, a "mobled" Queen), lays a wreath upon her own coffin.

From now on the fearful event races past. The duel scene. Its daggers, its potions, its deaths. The death fall of the poisoned Queen. The ebbing of Hamlet's life, haunted by the Gravedigger-Yorick image.

And the return of the opening theme played to muffled drums as the body of Hamlet is borne off, on the shoulders of Fortinbras' Four Captains Helpmannised into four monks, hooded and gowned—dramatically right for the hoods and gowns are more theatrically effective for bearers than the coal-scuttles and fire-guard accoutrement which was the military equipment of the period (*vide* the Old Vic).

This, then, is the spine of the ballet that has given rise to so much discussion. I personally regret the hovering Horatio who is so comfortable a presence in the play.

But again Helpmann's omissions have been those of the experienced hand. There is nothing tentative about *Hamlet*. All has been foreseen and everything dovetailed.

* It has to be admitted that at the first performance of the work, when poor wander-witted Ophelia advanced down stage to play with her fingers and bite her brother's ear, an insignificant member of the audience, who shall be nameless, observed to her neighbour with a gesture in the direction of the vast field of action which is Mr. Hurry's backcloth: "All This and Incest, Too!" . . .

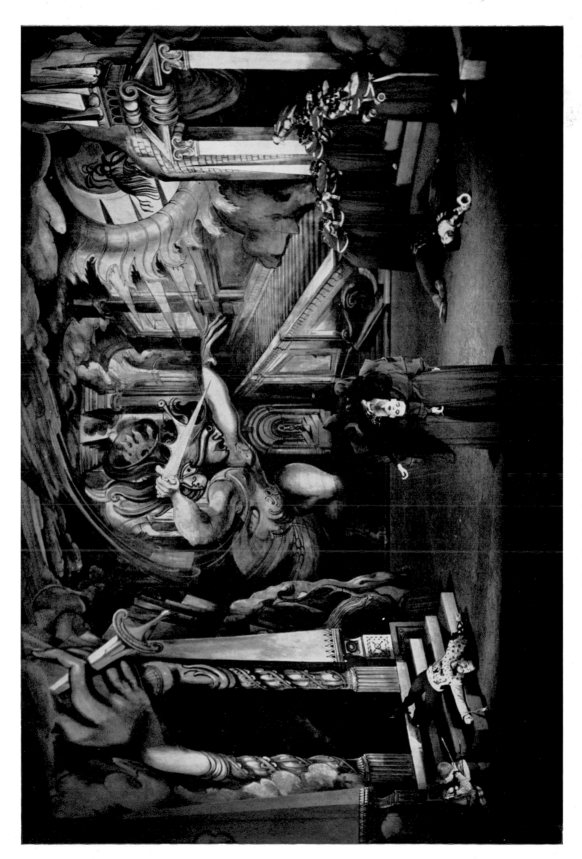

31. The beginning and the end of Helpmann's *Hamlet*

32.   Gravedigger-Yorick duplication from Helpmann's *Hamlet*

33.   Alas, poor Yorick! A fellow of infinite jest.

34. That skull had a tongue in it and could sing, once.

The ballet-goer has been overwhelmingly enthusiastic.* And the greater part of the responsible press has been impressed.

The New Statesman and Nation felt the ballet to be a "striking success".

"It is as different, in conception and technique, from *Comus* as one can imagine. No speeches this time, no formal episodes, none of the attitude of pale sickly thought that might have been anticipated, but a single swift scene in which the main events and the conflicts of the play flicker to and fro as they might in the brain of a dying man. The curtain rises on the tableau of tragedy with which Shakespeare ends; Hamlet has been hoisted aloft on the shoulders of four pall-bearers; his last moments of consciousness, the dream carried into eternity, are then enacted, and the pall-bearers slowly move away. Mime rather than dancing gives the texture of this phantasmagoria. Its elements—the ghost in armour, Yorick's skull, the King and Queen, Ophelia drowned, Hamlet himself spurred to action and tormented by nightmare—are already known to us, so that a few gestures or a confrontation can evoke whole scenes. This understanding on the part of the audience is important because it enables Mr. Helpmann to elaborate a ballet which is both complex and swift and to vary his theme audaciously. Some of the detail is brilliant; the moment, for instance, when the figures of Gertrude and Ophelia merge and divide before the distracted gaze of Hamlet. Ophelia, indeed, beautifully danced by Margot Fonteyn, acquires a new significance. Not only do the sweetness and madness go better to dance, but other aspects emerge; her attachment to Laertes is almost as strong as Hamlet's love for his mother. Helpmann's Hamlet is at all times the centre of lurid drama and shifting pattern, and his performance magnificently holds the eye. The music selected from Tchaikovsky† and the décor by Leslie Hurry add to the tension. The whole ballet, in fact, triumphs in regions somewhat painfully explored by the Expressionists, Evreinov and others, and achieves what they miss: interior drama that shall also be dramatic. The *Hamlet* at the New Theatre combines ballet, Grand Guignol and an exciting critical postscript to Shakespeare's play. Mr. Helpmann has such a variety of gifts that it is impossible to guess which way he will turn next."

The Dancing Times, however, takes quite another view of Helpmann's experiment:

* One correspondent wrote to Mr. Helpmann: "I want you to know how very much I have enjoyed your new ballet. As I have many times said to my husband, 'Hamlet always has been ruined by the words'."
† In fact, the music is Tchaikovsky's Hamlet Overture Fantasia.

"This is not a balletised version of the play, but an impression of the dreams that come to Hamlet as his spirit leaves his dead body. The ballet opens with the removal of his corpse from the courtyard of the castle and closes with the same episode. In between we are given a nightmarish picture of certain outstanding events of his life.

After he had composed the music of the Overture, Tchaikovsky was not entirely satisfied and wrote to a friend that he feared he had not caught the spirit of Hamlet, and my first hurried impression after an initial visit to this ballet is that the choreographer has similarly failed.

As one reads the quotation of the famous soliloquy which Mr. Helpmann has taken for his inspiration—'For in that sleep of death what dreams may come, When we have shuffled off this mortal coil, Must give us pause'—one decides that there is scope for endless possibilities. But if one reads through the soliloquy it is quickly realised that Shakespeare laid down exactly what Hamlet would see in his dreams. Shakespeare was a realist and a true servant of the theatre, understanding that clarity of characterisation was one of its first demands. Shakespeare's Hamlet was sane and he studied his every movement; he certainly did not succeed in carrying out his ideas of vengeance until the final scene, but this was because of certain superstitious doubts within himself.

Helpmann's Hamlet is not the dream of a sane man. He has presented, in some cases, the actual action of Shakespeare's play and interjected figments from his own imagination of what might have been. This makes the mimodrama (one can scarcely call it 'ballet') extremely difficult to follow at a first visit, because this Hamlet does not logically think out his actions as does Shakespeare's. The latter also realised that intense drama must be leavened with lighter touches. Such touches are entirely missing from this *Hamlet*.

In the name-part Robert Helpmann proves what a very fine dramatic actor he is and he receives excellent support from the company in this direction, but one hopes that future productions by the Wells will not relegate dancing to such a subordinate position. Mr. Hurry's costumes were beautiful, but his backcloth suggested that a portion of the castle had also 'shuffled off the mortal coil' and entered the region of the nightmare."

Very respectfully the writer of these pages takes issue with the distinguished critic of *The Dancing Times*. I submit that the worst possible approach to Mr. Helpmann's ballet is a detailed reading of Shakespeare's soliloquies. Mr. Helpmann is concerned with the staging of a ballet and not with the philosophical content of the Shakespearean passages. I submit that the distinguished critic would be the first to complain if the choreographer had given the ballet a "literary" tendency. And that it is in the freedom of its adaptation, and in the placing of the event after Shakespeare's play has finished, that Helpmann's Hamlet gets its fluent balletic quality and its emotional and dramatic strength.

Moreover, the distinguished critic specifically states that Shakespeare, "a realist and a true servant of the theatre," laid down "exactly what Hamlet would see". But did he? I submit that Shakespeare was far too great a realist to risk speculation upon that split second of racing recollection in any than the most general terms and figures.

Let us digress to examine a death scene—perhaps the most moving of any—from another play: Falstaff's passing from *King Henry the Fifth*.

"A' made a finer end, and went away, an it had been any christom child; a' parted ev'n just between twelve and one, ev'n at the turning o' th' tide: for after I saw him fumble with the sheets, and play with flowers, and smile upon his finger ends, I knew there was but one way; for his nose was as sharp as a pen, and a' babbled of green fields. 'How now, Sir John!' quoth I: 'what, man! Be o' good cheer.' So a' cried out 'God, God, God!' three or four times. Now I, to comfort him, bid him a' should not think of God; I hoped there was no need to trouble himself with any such thoughts yet. So a' bade me lay more clothes on his feet; I put my hand into the bed and felt them, and they were as cold as any stone; then I felt to his knees, and they were cold as any stone; and so upward and upward, and all was as cold as any stone."

Yes, Shakespeare was a realist. But there is no sign here of any guesses as to a racing phantasmagoria in a dying man's mind.

But Mr. Helpmann is not a realist. The terms of his art-medium do not admit of realism. Mr. Helpmann is not even a surrealist—e.g. a romantic realist in love with irreconcilable objects. He is a romanticist, with an emotional attraction towards the dramatic. And I submit that it is fitting that he should approach his subject balletically, dramatically, and, if he feels that way about it, melodramatically. And if, in the telling of his tale, the dancing cadenza is at all times subservient to the express unfolding of his story, this is a new aspect of Ballet—not a bad aspect of Ballet.

In a subsequent issue, however, the distinguished critic of *The Dancing Times* suffers a change of heart.

"After seeing *Hamlet* for a second time it becomes increasingly evident that Helpmann has given us an outstanding production, brilliantly interpreted by the company, which will appeal to a very large public. Call it *mimodrama* and the only debatable point is his treatment of the mentality of Hamlet: let us leave that to the Shakespearean *savants*. Call it a ballet and one is faced with a ballet in which dancing, the principal ingredient of ballet, is scarcely present. This lack of dance is due to the quality of Tchaikovsky's music, which depicts the climax of each episode but does not paint the action leading up to that climax. Modern choreographers for the most part endeavour to achieve a convincing parallel between the music selected and the dance created. Mr. Helpmann has drawn this parallel, but he could not create dance because the music does not demand it. It is hoped that having made this experiment the Wells will remember that when we go to see them we go to see dancing."

But even with this revised verdict the present writer is, very respectfully, at variance. Mr. Helpmann does not "create dance", not because the music "does not admit of it"—it is free and flowing, and indeed there are some dance passages—but because the dramatic sweep of events does not admit of dancing cadenza as such.

Does the distinguished critic fall foul of Fokine when Petrouchka in his cell fails to avail himself of the distraught *entrechat dix* (Nijinsky created Petrouchka) or the licentious *tour en l'air?*

Surely it is time—and high time—that the dancing cadenza be relegated to a position of interest subservient to, rather than in competition with, the plot, or have we seen the work of Fokine, Massine and Balanchine to no purpose?

The distinguished critic has turned, in these passages, from being Mr. Helpmann's indicter to his apologist. This shows an elasticity of judgment that is rare and valuable in a critic. But I beg to submit that the way to justify the choreographer is not to throw the blame on some other element of the work under discussion, but rather to consider what we stand to lose dramatically by a too slavish devotion to the Ballerina (or Danseur) as centre-piece.

Punch takes a better view of the work: Hamlet is "extremely effective".

35.   List, list, oh list!

36.   I could a tale unfold,
   Make thy two eyes, like stars, start from their spheres.

"We have long known of Mr. Helpmann's versatility and ability to portray the tragic, the sinister and the macabre, and this subject gives him the fullest scope . . . the atmosphere of blood and horror is admirably sustained by the gory-looking décor, with its clutching hands and dripping daggers."

The Times stresses the musical aspect of the work:

"Mr. Robert Helpmann's new ballet on the theme of *Hamlet* is based on the music of Tchaikovsky rather than on the play by Shakespeare. Any other course for the choreographer would be impossible, for his designs are drawn from the symphonic-poem which forms the musical half of the composite art of ballet. The music has nothing to do with Shakespeare's sequence of events, so the ballet cannot follow the scenes.* . . . It is cleverly staged and danced, though dancing properly so-called is not much concerned in the total effect."

The Observer was enthusiastic:

"Robert Helpmann's new ballet, *Hamlet*, is likely to be as warmly discussed as it was heartily applauded at the New Theatre on Tuesday night. It is a first-rate piece of imaginative theatre, excitingly assembled, brilliantly decorated and appropriately tuned. . . .

A striking virtue of this new work is the theatrical mastery and reconciliation of its prime elements—drama, music and decoration. It has a passionate homogeneity. Leslie Hurry's scenery and costumes have strong individuality and are highly effective. Tchaikovsky's music is a congenial solvent. The interest is cumulative. A complete contrast in key to his *Comus*, this new work advances Mr. Helpmann's reputation and reflects true glory on the Sadler's Wells Ballet, and on the dancers he and Margot Fontcyn so brilliantly lead."

The Manchester Guardian refuses to be flummoxed:

"At the New Theatre last night the Sadler's Wells Ballet Company presented a florid twenty minutes of mime and music entitled *Hamlet;* music by Tchaikovsky, costumes and décor by Leslie Hurry, choreography by Robert Helpmann. Characters, as you may have guessed, by Shakespeare, and finally cheers by a crowded house.

* The ballet-goer has only to recall the recent choreographical adaptation of another play by Shakespeare, *Twelfth Night*, to music by Grieg, with choreography by Andrée Howard, which does follow the Shakespearean sequence of scenes, to realise how unballetic a literal adaptation can be.—C. B.

There was no need to be alarmed. *Hamlet* has survived modern dress, Sir Henry Irving, Ambrose Thomas and Dr. Bowdler; and if a ballet-master chooses to translate it into terms of *The Yellow Book*, Shakespeare can take it with head unbowed. . . .

It is all very daring, but the spirit of ballet has done bolder things than this, and here it succeeds by creating an imaginative unity of style and matter, of emotion and action, of scene and music. Even Tchaikovsky proved to be in the picture, for his music helped to warm the air of fervid, convulsive romance in which the whole was presented. Mr. Helpmann was again happy in his favourite part of a young man in the throes."

The Queen recorded:

"The Sadler's Wells Company's new ballet at the New Theatre is as lovely as any of their productions, plus a strangeness, a successfully captured dream quality, that makes it specially memorable.

Robert Helpmann is choreographer, but it is mime, tableaux, and drama rather than ballet; so it might be said that Robert Helpmann devised it, brilliantly combining beauty with a penetrating psychology, imagination with professional stagecraft.

The quintessence of Hamlet is expressed in this picture of his subconscious, the whole of his life is telescoped into this performance of a dream or nightmare. . . .

Leslie Hurry's surrealist décor is magnificent, also his costumes. . . .

The Tchaikovsky overture to *Hamlet*, which has been used as it stood, is a gift to Mr. Helpmann's purpose."

The Daily Telegraph made it the subject of its Saturday musical leader:

"Quite apart from music written specially for it, the ballet has found compositions almost miraculously adapted to its purposes. Chopin's and Schumann's works, for instance, have been fitted so well that they might have been meant originally for the choreographer.*

Hamlet, which has now been added to the Sadler's Wells repertory, is less fortunate in this respect. In its general character Tchaikovsky's score fits the action well enough. It is eminently dramatic, and thus suited to a set of incidents which after a brief quarter of an hour end by the demise of half a dozen characters—an achievement the Grand Guignol might find it difficult to rival.

Some episodes, on the other hand, revealed a certain discrepancy between music and action. Had Tchaikovsky meant to give us his version

---

* *Les Sylphides* and *Carnaval*, it is to be supposed.—C. B.

36

of the Ghost scene he would, one felt, have written something different from the music which introduced the very substantial Ghost of the ballet.

So, too, Ophelia's madness, the play within the play, had these come within the scope of his work, would have resulted in something appropriate, characteristic, and rather different from the music heard at the New Theatre.

No doubt the relation between music and mimed action need not be as close as that between music and song. As the first night reception of the ballet showed, the audience found in Mr. Helpmann's choreography all the compensation it needed for the loss of the poetry and philosophy associated with the play. It might, however, be worth while to pay closer attention to the musical score when contemplating new productions."

Once again the writer of these pages, very respectfully, takes issue with a distinguished critic: whatever the colour and quality of the theme he wrote for it, Tchaikovsky did indeed indicate the "very substantial ghost" of the ballet, "armed at point, exactly cap-à-pie". He even noted on his score that this was a warrior ghost.

"No doubt the relation between music and mimed action need not be as close as that between music and song," observes the learned critic, broadmindedly.

Again I beg to take issue.

The relation of mimed action (as an element of the dance) bears as close a relation as at least the voice bears to the music of the song. Certain freedoms of phrasing must be allowed the mime, just as the singer or the instrumentalist. But dance is as closely linked to music in the instrumentation of a ballet as instruments are linked to a score. That is why the choreographic addition to a symphony is doomed to artistic failure from the point of view of the purist in balletics. The musical development, repetition and climaxes put too great a strain on the physical medium of the choreographer. He cannot adequately reflect orchestral thought, length, idiom and treatment within the statement of his own art.

But in my view Mr. Helpmann has not strained the resources of his expression in the choreography devised to the score of the Overture Fantasy, nor has he in any way violated the spirit of the Tchaikovsky score. What he has done has been to combine the score which Tchaikovsky wrote after witnessing a performance of *Hamlet* with Shakespeare's play, and add to both some comments from his own age.

To convey a situation or mood in a manner which conveys a comment

37

is a part of the true function of Ballet. If not, let us revert to *divertissements* and have done with an art-form.

To his critics Helpmann has himself replied in an article—really the report of a speech made to members of the Royal Academy of Dancing—published in *The Dancing Times:*

> "A ballet, like a play, is an elastic medium which must be used by each creator in an individual way. . . . Mime is as legitimate a medium in the element of Ballet as dancing; in fact, what distinguishes the choreography from an arrangement of dance-steps is its concentration on the composition as a whole—not merely the dance movements, but also the mime.
>
> To have attempted to treat either of my dramatic subjects, *Comus* or *Hamlet*, in terms of *fouettés* and *entrechats* would have been completely wrong, both dramatically and musically, but to exclude a choreographic dramatic rendering of such subjects because they demand a larger element of mime than pure dancing seems to me to be dangerously limiting the scope of the Ballet as a whole . . .
>
> I speak now, not only for myself, but for all modern choreographers. For many years I have watched the critic of modern Ballet always ready to say 'very nice, very dramatic, very beautifully presented, but no dancing'. What do they mean by 'no dancing'? No fifth positions, perhaps, no pirouettes, perhaps, no *entrechats* perhaps—but dancing. Every movement made on the stage by a dancer must be dancing. Even to walk across the stage is, I find, to the average dancer, often more difficult than a set of *brisés*—and impossible for the average actor.
>
> I am sure that if the modern Ballet critic could attend more rehearsals of Ballets and learn to understand the reason for modern Ballet there would be less mistaken criticism of Ballet to-day."

All credit to *The Dancing Times* for its fair treatment of much that must go against the editorial grain. All credit to Robert Helpmann for his moderation in writing of the ballet criticism of to-day.

The present writer would like to go one stage further and to suggest that a greater attendance in the class-rooms, where the dancers work and correct their mistakes, is an imperative necessity for all who record and comment in the Press upon their performances.

37. Ophelia-Gertrude duplication from Helpmann's *Hamlet*

38. The Queen-Ophelia duplication in a still from Helpmann's *Hamlet*

Helpmann's choreography for *Hamlet* is simple and effective, made from movement which fits thought like a glove. Even Hamlet's *pas seuls* are simple and thought-racked instead of being complex and textually digressional as are so many dancing passages in dramatic ballets. And Helpmann, in dancing these transposed soliloquies, gives them a pace, a sweep of emotion, and an articulated elegance such as a Gielgud gives to the spoken lines.

Living, Hamlet was torn and racked with indecision. Dying, the fever, the turgid suspicions and the awful fulfilments telescope into a fierce purposefulness that ends in a blood-bath.

Mr. Hurry's décor emphasises the blood-bath aspect.

His decadent palace (Plate 48), with its dramatic staircase and its cold carven aisles, is the very place for a nice spot of bother. The great vengeful figure, the hand with the dagger,* and all the rushing drama of the painted scene prepare the mind for dread event. Black Hamlet is surrounded but never overpowered by the scarlet fusion.

And the costumes—elaborate, fantasticated, slashed and braided—are beautifully balanced and serve both dancer and choreographer both by preserving the line of arm and leg and by lending to the groups an added emphasis. (See Plates 31, 4, 44 and 45.)

Indeed, as Mr. Hurry foresaw, it took a garment with a wealth of detail to draw the eye from the great backcloth and claim the fullest attention for the dancer.

Ophelia is perhaps the least successful of Mr. Helpmann's figures in this ballet. Shakespeare's Ophelia is pliant and simple. Helpmann's Ophelia (and that of Margot Fonteyn) is scheming and at times a little harsh. Harsh in her madness and touched with the Queen's own magnetism in the Queen-Ophelia duplication.†

Ophelia is most successful when she is shrouded in her river, drowned from the top of her Pinchbeck crown to the tips of her green satin slippers in falling folds of blue water—an effective and balletic conception. (Plates 48 and 51.)

---

* What will Mr. Hurry have left for the embellishment of Macbeth?

† The writer overheard the following fascinating snatch of conversation in the foyer after the first performance of *Hamlet* as a ballet:

Baffled Blonde: "Was she bats, darling?"

Her Escort: "Completely cuckoo, darling."

Baffled Blonde: "Of course I've read *Hamlet* more than once but I don't remember a thing about Ophelia. . . ."

In Shakespeare's *Hamlet*, Gertrude, the Queen, is an amiable but silly woman. It is the King who is the villain of the piece. Helpmann's duplications, and the personal beauty of Celia Franca who dances the Queen, put a different emphasis upon the play's characterisations: the Queen flowers triumphantly upon her second marriage like a lovely evil orchid, while the King dwindles to a puppet's stature with a puppet's potentialities. (Plate 45.)

The Ghost stalks the stage bringing his sufferings home to our bones, and the Gravedigger nimbles in the action's crevices. (Plates 34 and 35.)

This, then, is the ballet that Sadler's Wells has produced in the middle of quite a war.

Even had it been created during the days of peace, it would still, in my view, have been the final vindication of the somewhat inbred system of that organisation.

39. Here's metal more attractive.

40. Group from *Hamlet*

41. Keep you in the rear of your affection,
Out of the shot and danger of desire.

42. 'Tis in my memory lockt,
And you yourself shall keep the key of it.

43. Look you, how cheerfully my mother looks.

44. Though this be madness, yet there's method in't!

45. Our sometime sister, now our Queen.

46. Helpmann as Hamlet

47.   For bonny sweet Robin is all my joy.

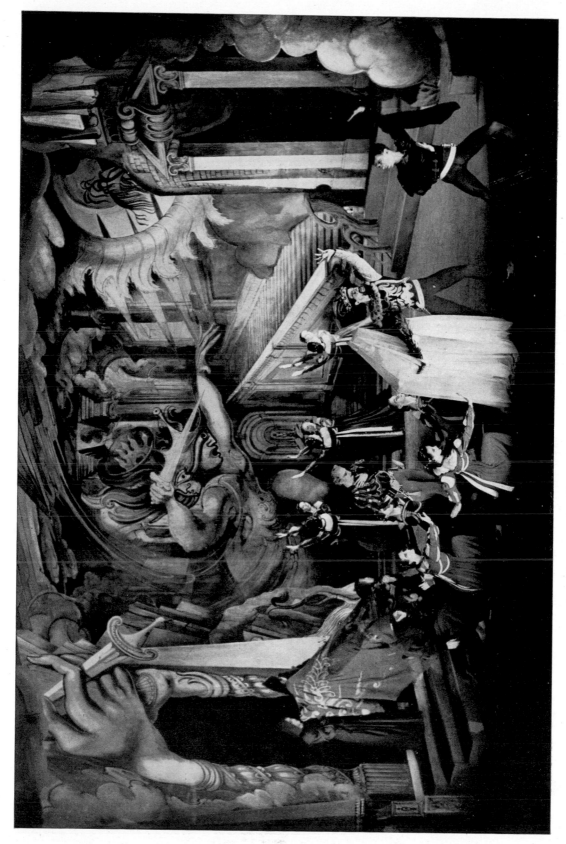

48. Drowned Ophelia bears a wreath to her own bier

49.   We may call it herb o' grace o' Sundays!

50. Hadst thou thy wits and didst persuade revenge,
It could not move thus!

51. Ophelia "mobled" in her river
Margot Fonteyn and Robert Helpmann

52.   Let's further think of this;
Weigh what convenience both of time and means
May fit us to our shape.

53. The devil take thy soul.

54. A Freudian Triangle

55. The Sparrows and the Hen at the beginning of *The Birds*: characterisations by Helpmann out of Disney

VIII

HELPMANN'S INVENTION begins to be seen in his third ballet—*The Birds*,
with décor and costumes by Chiang Yee to music by Respighi founded
upon works by composers of the 17th & 18th centuries. In this work his
disinclination to put in an accustomed *pas* if it does not perfectly convey
the emotion or purpose of the dancer is clearly marked. Indeed, it is the
integrity that keeps him from the dancing *cliché* which raises the little work
from the ranks of "first ballets" (those dim, rather dreary little works, shorn
of their principals and long bereft of their earlier fire, that serve to persuade
the house, in some measure, to stop talking) and places it among the
sophisticated company of slight works worth arriving in time to see.

For *The Birds*, for all its apparent simplicity, is a sophisticated little
ballet.

It is, in fact, the love story of the Nightingale and the Dove.

The Dove loves the Nightingale who sings so sweetly in the forest. The
cackling Hen loves the Dove. She disguises herself as her rival, mainly by
borrowing her steps—for this is true ballet—and endeavours to charm the
Dove. The Cuckoo loves the Nightingale. He borrows the Dove's plumage
and endeavours to charm the Nightingale. The Hen mistakes the Cuckoo
for the Dove. The Cuckoo mistakes the Hen for the Nightingale. The
Nightingale and the Dove come radiantly together. And two sparrows help
the audience to enjoy the joke.

The theme, it will be seen, is balletic. The treatment it receives is unexpected. In fact, there is very little of anything that you may have grown
to expect, in this ballet. Not the least is the cardinal fact that, though a
Helpmann work, it is not without the purely dancing cadenza. All the
ingredients are a little different from what the ballet-goer expects them
to be, always excepting the music. So that for the first time in the recollection of this particularly hardened ballet-goer she came away from the
performance too divided between the work's merits and its faults to trust
her instant judgment.

First the set: a painted backcloth of a flashing and glowing green forest
is what you expect to find, not in the Ballet, but in the illustrations to a

book. In its favour it can be said that so must a leafy forest glow and flash to the eye of a bird. Indeed, it reduces the audience to beady-eyed bird-attentiveness, snatching at our interests now at this point, now that, drawing us always away from the dancer and detracting from the dancing line. (Plate 67.)

The choreographer has brought on the Dove and his attendant cooing court from behind a fence, instead of giving it the freedom of passage of the Nightingale, so that our Hero arrives, as it were, in the centre of a travelling scrum.

The Hen is a figure, animated by a lesser Disney. (Plate 56.)

The distinguished dancer, Doubrovska, at the time when she was dancing the Fire-bird for Diaghilev and the Enchantress in the Balanchine *Fils Prodigue*, might adequately have danced the Nightingale. But Beryl Grey, though she brings to the part a taking personal radiance, lacks precision and has not yet that mastery of technique that makes a technical passage anything more than a series of dilemmas light-heartedly survived. (Plate 57.)

What, then, is it that has drawn the writer of these pages to the New Theatre over and over again when this ballet has been given? Oddly enough, the answer is the dancing interest.

Helpmann's avoidance of the dancing *cliché* has given his *enchainements* a new interest.

The *fouetté*, when it becomes the spun song of the Nightingale (if performed, as it were, on a postage-stamp and not in control of the dancer sending her spinning across the stage), is a delight. The arabesque, when it implies flight, takes on a new loveliness. Helpmann has found a new choreography for the Attendant Doves. It features a minimum of flutter-fingers and a charming snuggling suggestion of the tender *roucoulement* in dovey throats. The plot is arranged clearly. It is simple and amusing. And it is set forth in a sophisticated manner. The characterisations are extremely deft. The whole ballet flashes with wit masquerading as broad humour.

In fact, of all the bird ballets this work gives a greater feeling of the bird, in flight and in song, than any—save for the opening series of *jettés ouvertes* of the Fire-bird in Fokine's *L'Oiseau de Feu;* an impression which is greatly strengthened by the flaming feathers of Goncharova's costume and the flash and dip in the Stravinsky score.

56. The Disney influence in *The Birds:* the Hen (Moya Fraser)

57: The Nightingale (Beryl Grey)

58. The Hen fails to console the melancholy Dove

59. *Entrée* of the Nightingale

60. Flight in the Forest

61. This group, from *The Birds*, resembles a Balanchine grouping

62. A *roucoulement* of Doves

63.   The Hen gets her Big Idea

64. Line and Balance in a group from *The Birds*

65. Flight in Ballet

66. Beryl Grey and Alexis Rassine: the Nightingale and the Dove

67.   The Nightingale and the Dove

68.   Birds in borrowed plumage: the Hen, heavily disguised as the
Nightingale, assumes her pose

69.   Blackmail among the Sparrows

70.   Flight in the Forest, again: a lovely study in line from *The Birds*
(Beryl Grey and Alexis Rassine)

IX

PEOPLE often ask me what Robert Helpmann is like as a person.

He is a man in love with the theatre.

This is the first thing to be said about Helpmann. I believe he would be content for it to be the last.

Printed at The Westminster Press
411a Harrow Road
London, W.9